JAMES

THEOLOGY ᴼᶠ WORK PROJECT

JAMES

THE BIBLE ᴬᴺᴰ YOUR WORK
Study Series

HENDRICKSON
PUBLISHERS

Theology of Work
The Bible and Your Work Study Series: James

© 2014 by Hendrickson Publishers Marketing, LLC
P.O. Box 3473
Peabody, Massachusetts 01961-3473

ISBN 978-1-61970-517-3

William Messenger, Executive Editor, Theology of Work Project
Sean McDonough, Biblical Editor, Theology of Work Project
Patricia Anders, Editorial Director, Hendrickson Publishers

Contributors:
Alison Gerber, "James" Bible Study
Kelly Liebengood and Al Erisman, "The General Epistles and Work" in the *Theology of Work Bible Commentary*

The Theology of Work Project is an independent, international organization dedicated to researching, writing, and distributing materials with a biblical perspective on work. The Project's primary mission is to produce resources covering every book of the Bible plus major topics in today's workplaces. Wherever possible, the Project collaborates with other faith-and-work organizations, churches, universities, and seminaries to help equip people for meaningful, productive work of every kind.

Printed in the United States of America

First Printing – November 2014

Contents

The Theology of Work   vii

1. Trust
Lesson #1: A Place to Start (James 1:1–8)   1

Lesson #2: It's Not about You (James 1:9–12)   4

Lesson #3: The Goodness of God (James 1:13–18)   8

2. What, Then, Shall We Do?
Lesson #1: Trust Leads to Obedience (James 1:22–25)   12

Lesson #2: What, Then, Shall We Do? (James 1:26–27)   15

Lesson #3: Finding Widows at Work (James 1:26–27)   17

3. Favoring the Wealthy, Ignoring the Rich
Lesson #1: What Does It Mean to Play Favorites?
(James 2:1–4)   21

Lesson #2: Two Arguments against Favoritism
(James 2:5–8)   24

Lesson #3: Favoritism Isn't Love (James 2:8–13)   27

4. Faith and Work(s)
Lesson #1: What Are Works? (James 2:14–17)   30

Lesson #2: Can Our Work Save Us? (James 2:14–26)   33

Lesson #3: Separating Faith and Work?
(James 2:18–26)   35

5. Speaking and Listening

Lesson #1: Learning to Listen Well (James 1:19–21)   39

Lesson #2: The Impossible Quest for Holy Speech
(James 3:1–8)   42

Lesson #3: Rejecting Two-Faced Behavior
(James 3:9–12)   43

6. Me vs. You

Lesson #1: "Wisdom" vs. Peace (James 3:13–18)   45

Lesson #2: Ambition vs. Submission (James 4:1–10)   48

Lesson #3: Slander vs. Love (James 4:11–12)   51

7. Two Warnings for the Wealthy

Lesson #1: We Don't Control the Future (James 4:13–17)   55

Lesson #2: We Must Not Hoard Wealth (James 5:1–4)   58

Lesson #3: Watching Out for Self-Indulgence
(James 5:5–6)   59

8. A Few Final Words of Advice

Lesson #1: Have Patience (James 5:7–11)   62

Lesson #2: Speak Truth (James 5:12)   65

Lesson #3: Get Specific (James 5:13–18)   67

Conclusion: Watch for the Wanderer (James 5:19–20)   71

Wisdom for Using This Study in the Workplace   75

Leader's Guide   77

The Theology of Work

Work is not only a human calling but also a divine one. "In the beginning God created the heavens and the earth." God worked to create us and created us to work. "The LORD God took the man and put him in the garden of Eden to till it and keep it" (Gen. 2:15). God also created work to be good, even if it's hard to see in a fallen world. To this day, God calls us to work to support ourselves and to serve others (Eph. 4:28).

Work can accomplish many of God's purposes for our lives—the basic necessities of food and shelter, as well as a sense of fulfillment and joy. Our work can create ways to help people thrive. Our work can discover the depths of God's creation. Our work can bring us into wonderful relationships with co-workers and those who benefit from our work (customers, clients, patients, and so forth).

Yet many people face drudgery, boredom, or exploitation at work. We have bad bosses, hostile relationships, and unfriendly work environments. Our work seems useless, unappreciated, faulty, frustrating. We don't get paid enough. We get stuck in dead-end jobs or laid off or fired. We fail. Our skills become obsolete. It's a struggle just to make ends meet. But how can this be if God created work to be good—and what can we do about it? God's answers to these questions must be somewhere in the Bible, but where?

The Theology of Work Project's mission has been to study what the Bible says about work and to develop resources to apply the Christian faith to our work. It turns out that every book of the Bible gives practical, relevant guidance that can help us do our jobs better, improve our relationships at work, support ourselves, serve others more effectively, and find meaning and value in our work. The Bible shows us how to live all of life—including work—in Christ. Only in Jesus can our work be transformed to become the blessing it was always meant to be.

To put it another way, if we are not following Christ during the 100,000 hours of our lives that we spend at work, are we really following Christ? Our lives are more than just one day a week at church. The fact is that God cares about our life *every day of the week*. But how do we become equipped to follow Jesus at work? In the same ways we become equipped for every aspect of life in Christ—listening to sermons, modeling our lives on others' examples, praying for God's guidance, and most of all by studying the Bible and putting it into practice.

This Theology of Work series contains a variety of books to help you apply the Scriptures and Christian faith to your work. This Bible study is one volume in the series The Bible and Your Work. It is intended for those who want to explore what the Bible says about work and how to apply it to their work in positive, practical ways. Although it can be used for individual study, Bible study is especially effective with a group of people committed to practicing what they read in Scripture. In this way, we gain from one another's perspectives and are encouraged to actually *do* what we read in Scripture. Because of the direct focus on work, The Bible and Your Work studies are especially suited for Bible studies *at* work or *with* other people in similar occupations. The following lessons are designed for thirty-minute lunch breaks, although they can be used in other formats as well.

Christians today recognize God's calling to us in and through our work—for ourselves and for those whom we serve. May God use this book to help you follow Christ in every sphere of life and work.

Will Messenger, Executive Editor
Theology of Work Project

Chapter 1

Trust

Lesson #1: A Place to Start (James 1:1–8)

James's original readers—"scattered among the nations" (James 1:1)—were facing "trials of many kinds" (1:2). They were living in countries that were struggling through political instability and famine, where loss of property and ethnic discrimination were common. There was friction in the church along class lines, and fractures among their once close communities were beginning to form.

Though our lives might be free from famine or the kind of ethnic and religious persecution these first-century Christians were facing, none of our lives is free from difficulty and neither are our workplaces. The twenty-first-century workplace is rife with stories of harassment, discrimination, bullying, and burnout. Like never before, workers face the fear of unemployment, underemployment, being underpaid, and of carrying the burden of an unreasonable workload. In many places of the world, corruption is a constant drain on prosperity, and we all face daily ethical challenges, no matter where we work. People at every level in our organizations cause problems for which we must find solutions. We have colleagues with whom we just can't seem to get along. We toil through long hours and yet continue to feel a lack of direction, purpose, or security at the core of our existence.

Into a world under pressure, Scripture speaks. James reminds these early believers, and us, that we can, and must, trust God to provide the wisdom we need to live through difficult and uncertain times.

 Food for Thought

What struggles are you facing right now in your workplace as we begin this study together? Spend some time listing these, and then ask God if he would—over the next few weeks as we dig into his word—breathe his wisdom into those areas of your life that need it.

_____

_____

_____

_____

_____

_____

_____

It can be a struggle to believe that God will provide what we need to overcome the real and present difficulties we face at work. James tells us that doubting God's provision is what leads to double-mindedness (1:8). Double-minded people are those unsure whether or not they are willing to trust God. In fact, double-minded people are those unsure whether or not they want to follow Jesus Christ.

A double-minded person is like a spinning coin, not yet fallen on the side of heads or tails. It's certainly not a desirable state to stay in forever. Double-mindedness leaves you "unstable" (1:8), not about "to receive anything from the Lord" (1:7), and "like a wave of the sea, blown and tossed by the wind" (1:6).

On the other hand, believing in God and trusting that he will provide you with the wisdom you need is the seed from which all good things are grown. It might seem hard to trust God at work, but consider the priority James gives by beginning his letter with these words, "If any of you lacks wisdom, you should ask God, who gives generously to all without finding fault, and it will be given to you" (1:5). Trusting God wholeheartedly that he will hear and answer our requests for help is an essential foundation of our faith, and one we can rely on every day of our working life.

 Food for Thought

Look back over the list of hardships you are facing at work. Is there any area of your work where you are not sure if God could possibly help? Remember that Christ waits patiently for you always, ready and eager to receive even the most meager trust in him.

_____

_____

_____

_____

_____

_____

_____

Prayer

Pause for a few moments of silence to reflect on what you've just studied. Then offer a prayer, either spontaneous or by using the following:

> *Father God, source of all wisdom,*
>
> *I come before you humbly to ask for that very wisdom to be at work in the difficulties I now face. Speak to me and help me. Please forgive me, Lord, for the areas of my life that I have not wholly entrusted to you. I commit those things to you now. I do believe that you will hear this prayer and will help me as I work for you.*
>
> *In Christ's name I pray, amen.*

Lesson #2: It's Not about You (James 1:9–12)

Have you ever held a "high position" (James 1:9)? Ever aced a presentation or a job interview? You can probably recall the electric feeling of being among a group of people turned to your favor—that sensation of all eyes in the room resting on you as they nod and smile in approval to every word you say. It's an incredible feeling to achieve success and gain recognition for your work.

Andy was the president of a start-up publishing company that had grown rapidly under his leadership. As a result it was purchased by a larger company, at great benefit to the start-up company's stockholders and employees. The business remained a separate entity under its new owner, and it continued to grow strongly. The new parent corporation added other businesses to Andy's unit, and he found that he had become one of two candidates to become CEO of the parent company. However, he preferred to continue leading his business unit, so he withdrew his name from consideration, and the other candidate was selected. Andy's unit continued to perform excellently, but after two years, the new CEO asked for his resignation. "My leadership style was very different from the new CEO's," Andy says, "and you really can't have the head of the largest division operate with a leadership style so different from the CEO's. So I had to go. No matter how successful you may be, some things are out of your control. It's just a fact of business."

Over time, it began to dawn on Andy that God had moved him out of his position for a reason—to give him time for other kinds of work. He helped establish The Kings College, a new Christian college in the heart of America's financial center, and helped guide it to excellence. He mentored a flock of executives and co-founded several ministries to help people apply their faith to the business world. His family life blossomed. "I worked hard both before and after I left the publishing industry," he says. "But it was only when I recognized that God is truly in charge—and tried to live my life in response—that I began to find the deepest purpose and satisfaction."

We often imagine that our success and our wealth are mainly due to our own effort. We pat ourselves on the back with each successful job application, new promotion, raise, or award. But James warns that if we depend primarily on our own ability, we will be caught off balance when circumstances change. Success or failure comes from many factors beyond us. Continuing to work with an "it's all about me" mind-set and failing to recognize our dependence on God only means that these things—great jobs, promotions, awards, and even wealth—will not last. The "blossom falls," says James (1:11). If not now, then certainly at the end of life.

 *Food for Thought*

Name a moment of success you've had recently in the workplace. Besides yourself, what other people, resources, and circumstances can you recognize as making that success possible? What about God? Spend some time now acknowledging God's part in that success. What gifts had he given you at birth that led to this point? What opportunities did he present you with recently, or even through your background and previous life experiences?

_____

_____

_____

_____

Conversely, what about when we as Christians face failure or financial struggle? When we find ourselves to be the victim of unfair work practices, theft, abuse, or discrimination? Is it right then to ask, "What did I do to deserve this?"

_____

_____

_____

_____

Anyone who has ever made a costly business decision or suddenly lost their life savings—whether through fraud, crop failure, illness, or recession—knows firsthand that there is much in the world outside of our control. Financial difficulties don't exist as marks of God's disfavor. On the contrary, we must continue to follow God faithfully through struggles and even economic hardship, success or failure at work, wealth or the lack of it in our lifetime. Most often these things are not *because* of us, but they are used by God *for* us. God uses success and failure and poverty and wealth to develop something that's really important—the perseverance we need to overcome evil and to attain "the crown of life that the Lord has promised to those who love him" (James 1:12).

 Food for Thought

Think back to a time of difficulty you went through at work, one for which you have now arrived at the other side. What has God taught you or developed in you through that time?

_____

_____

_____

_____

_____

_____

_____

_____

Prayer

Pause for a few moments of silence to reflect on what you've just studied. Then offer a prayer, either spontaneous or by using the following:

Father God, ruler of heaven and earth,

*I acknowledge that all things are under your control and
not mine. When success comes, help me to understand
that I am not the master of my own destiny but a humble
servant of yours. Help me in the hard times to keep my
eyes focused on the day when you will lift me up. Grow
perseverance in me, Lord. More than anything, more than
success, more than wealth, I want your crown of life—I
want to live with you forever.*

In Christ's name I pray, amen.

Lesson #3: The Goodness of God (James 1:13–18)

Remember the last time you were under pressure at work? Did
it drive you to your knees in search of God's help, or did it form
in you a stew of frustration and anger at your colleagues? When
we're facing hardship, we don't always respond by trusting God
and seeking his guidance to transform our lives. Instead, we
often blame others for our problems. "I had no choice" is the
oft-spoken slogan of sin.

James puts the responsibility for our failure to trust God squarely
back on our shoulders. "But each person is tempted when they
are dragged away by their own evil desire and enticed" (James
1:14). Sin isn't God's handiwork. It isn't a product of an external
mechanism but an internal one. It is a rift that runs through each
and every one of our own hearts. When we blame others for our
failings, we deceive ourselves. Then we see no reason to turn to
God for help in life or work.

Christians are not excluded from this problem. In fact, James's letter addresses *Christians*—men and women of the church. No one is exempt from the problem of sin, and church scandals and business frauds alike should remind us of that. Temptation and sin come from deep within the heart of us all.

 Food for Thought

What is a temptation you are facing right now? Brainstorm ways you might be able to prevent yourself from being "dragged away" and "enticed."

_____

_____

_____

_____

_____

_____

_____

While none of us is free from the temptation to sin, we do find solace in the incredible, almost unfathomable knowledge that we have a God who is wonderfully and limitlessly good. While out of our hearts comes our own evil desire, God is the "Father of the heavenly lights" (James 1:17)—meaning that he created the sun, moon, and stars and that he has the power and goodness to bring forth life and continuously sustain his creation.

Not only is God good, but he is also generous with his goodness. He is the giver of "every good and perfect gift" (James 1:17). Everything good we have in our lives has come to us from him, including our salvation. Through his goodness, he "chose to give us birth through the word of truth" (1:18). Out of his goodness, he chose to save us from wallowing in our doubt and self-importance and sin.

God's goodness creates a community of people who also seek to do good. They become like the very first neon sign hung in Times Square in New York City, an indication of a bright future, lit up with goodness, excitement, and activity—first of all shining in the world through his Son Jesus Christ.

 Food for Thought

God has been good to us, in giving us both new spiritual life and our employment. How might we be generous to others with the gifts God has graciously bestowed?

_____

_____

_____

_____

_____

_____

_____

_____

Prayer

Pause for a few moments of silence to reflect on what you've just studied. Then offer a prayer, either spontaneous or by using the following:

Creator God,

I acknowledge that I am the author of my sin. I am sorry for the times I have not followed your direction for my life and instead chosen to chase the desires of my heart. Help me to resist temptation. I acknowledge that you are indeed the author of my salvation and the bringer of all good things into my life. Shape me to be like you—wonderfully surprising and generously good.

In Christ's name I pray, amen.

Chapter 2

What, Then, Shall We Do?

Lesson #1: Trust Leads to Obedience (James 1:22–25)

Being created anew by God's goodness and trusting in his desire to help us should have a direct consequence on how we live. "Do not merely listen to the word" (1:22), says James, but rather "do what it says" (1:23).

When a business recognizes they have a serious gap in their abilities, they often hire expert consultants. Consultancy, however, is effective only if the business operators find their advice to be sound and put their changes into effect. In the same way, when we trust God, when we hear his instruction to us, the logical next step is to act on it—wholly accepting his plans as the right course of action for our lives.

 Food for Thought

Think of a person with whom you work whose advice you really trust. What would it take for you for your relationship with God to be just like that?

_____

_____

_____

_____

_____

_____

_____

_____

The connection between our actions and our trust is essential not coincidental. If we are not following God's direction, it probably indicates a lack of trust in him.

When we hear clear instruction from God with regard to our behavior or life direction, and yet refuse to respond, it is usually because we think we know better. We think we know better how to care for ourselves, and we think we know better how to get what we want. Perhaps we are even afraid—afraid that God does not have our best interests at heart, or afraid that he will fail to provide what we need.

We must, however, remember that *God is good*. Every good and perfect thing comes from him. He is worthy of your trust. "Do not merely listen to the word, and so deceive yourselves," James tells us (1:22). Trusting in God means doing what you hear him ask you to do. As you trust him, hear his call to respond to his guidance for your life.

Food for Thought

Where do you feel God's Spirit is leading you right now? What is he urging you to change or do in your workplace? If you don't know, how and when might you spend time this week *listening* to his word?

_____

_____

_____

_____

_____

_____

_____

Prayer

Pause for a few moments of silence to reflect on what you've just studied. Then offer a prayer, either spontaneous or by using the following:

> *Father God,*
>
> *Thank you that you haven't left your sheep without a shepherd, that you continue to speak to us and guide us even today. I am sorry, Lord, for the times I have refused to listen to your word, when I have failed to put my trust in you. Speak to me now. I am listening. I am looking for you to guide me as I work. Please help me, by the power of your Spirit, to trust you—not only to listen to your word but also to do what it says.*
>
> *In Christ's name I pray, amen.*

Lesson #2: What, Then, Shall We Do? (James 1:26–27)

If trust in God is revealed through obedience to his word, then the next logical step is to find out what the Lord is asking us to do. James offers three suggestions for a life lived in obedience to God in this passage. First is to keep a tight rein on our tongues (1:26). Second is to look after widows and orphans in their distress (1:27). Third is "to keep oneself from being polluted by the world" (1:27). James will unpack each of these in more detail, as will we in the proceeding chapters of this study.

 Food for Thought

Which of the three acts of obedience listed above poses the greatest challenge to you at this time?

_____

_____

_____

_____

_____

_____

_____

Imagine you have a big proposal due and the deadline is Friday. You've been working on it steadily and feel that, at the current rate of progress, by the week's end you will have achieved something really spectacular, perhaps even promotion-worthy. But then Brian, the new hire in the office next door, who is drowning under his workload (so much so that he might not keep his job), asks for an entire afternoon's worth of your help. Do you give it to him?

When we come across the needs of others, if we do *not* show any interest in meeting those needs, if we are solely focused on working only for our own benefit, this might be an indication that we aren't trusting God as our provider. Failure to work for others comes out of a lack of trust in God. Working for others, caring for others' needs, reveals a great trust in God's ability to care for us.

What does this have to do with widows and orphans? In James's time, widows and orphans were the extreme version of our floundering new colleague—the people of the greatest helplessness and need. Without family or any social welfare system to protect or provide for them, where could they turn? Yet God declared himself to be "a father to the fatherless, a defender of widows" (Ps. 68:5). As we care for the needy and helpless among us, not only are we trusting that God will take care of our needs, but we are also doing his very work.

 Food for Thought

Can you think of a time recently at work when you put your own needs ahead of someone else's? What need were you trying to meet? Do you believe that God could take care of that need?

_____

_____

_____

_____

_____

_____

Prayer

Pause for a few moments of silence to reflect on what you've just studied. Then offer a prayer, either spontaneous or by using the following:

> *Father God,*
>
> *You know I desire to do your will. Help me to cast off my fears and trust you completely. I want to let go of the desire to meet my own needs myself. Instead, help me to start to work for the needs of others, even today. Bring to me your people who are in need, open doors for me that I might do your work, serving them.*
>
> *In Christ's name I pray, amen.*

Lesson #3: Finding Widows at Work (reread James 1:26–27)

We will spend this lesson continuing to reflect on the practical implications of what we have just learned.

Every successful organization is characterized by this one attribute—its ability to meet another's needs. Whether it be customers, employees, shareholders, students, or clients, the degree to which a business meets needs effectively is a true measure of its success.

While James's attention is fixated on the needs of the most helpless and most needy, we can extrapolate another possible application from these verses—that where an organization is meeting a *true* need of humanity (as opposed to a manufactured need or a sinful desire), that organization is beginning to put earthly hands to the work of God, who is greatly concerned with meeting the needs of the world.

However, the act of meeting the needs of the "widows and or-phans" among us calls for great creativity on the part of the Christian in the marketplace, since the truly poor are too poor to be customers of an established business, and the truly powerless won't ever come knocking on the door of a corner office. For any business to meet widows and orphans with their work requires initiative. They must be actively pursued.

Followers of Jesus are taking up this challenge. Consider a group of Christians who started a furniture factory in Vietnam, provid-ing fair paying jobs for Vietnamese people at the lowest end of the socioeconomic spectrum. While the furniture they supply meets the need of their overseas customers, it also provides for the needs of the local people. Previously, they were desperately unemployed. Now God provides for these people through the work of his followers and this humble factory.

 Food for Thought

Who are the poor and powerless in your workplace? Who are the poor and powerless beyond those in your workplace whom your work affects? How might you, through your work, actively seek out the poor and powerless in order to better meet their needs?

_____

_____

_____

_____

_____

_____

A Christian's duty does not end with serving the poor and powerless through our work. Social, political, and economic systems
also strongly affect whether or not the needs of the poor are met.
Is it really acceptable for us as Christians, who are charged with
the responsibility to care for widows and orphans, who know
that these are on the heart of God himself, to stand by in situations where these systems benefit only the rich and powerful?
In as much as we have influence, we have a responsibility as followers of Jesus Christ to see that the needs of the helpless are
provided for through these structures and systems.

 Food for Thought

Have you recently come across an issue of the poor or powerless
being unjustly treated by our social, economic, or political system? How might you fight for their support financially, or with
your time through writing letters, or adjusting how you vote, or
even how you spend your money? What influence do you have
at or through your work, and how could you use it to serve the
poor and powerless?

_____

_____

_____

_____

_____

_____

_____

_____

Prayer

Pause for a few moments of silence to reflect on what you've just studied. Then offer a prayer, either spontaneous or by using the following:

Father God, Father of the fatherless and defender of the widow,

I know that you care for the widows and the orphans of the world. Where they might be hidden from me, help me to see them and see their need. Help me to come in contact with the poor and needy at work, and may my work provide for their needs. Make a way for me that I might be able to bring justice to their lives—to defend the ones you defend, to fight for those for whom you fight, to love the ones for whom you pour out your love.

In Christ's name I pray, amen.

Chapter 3

Favoring the Wealthy, Ignoring the Rich

Lesson #1: What Does It Mean to Play Favorites? (James 2:1–4)

At the time when James was writing, the early church was struggling to make ends meet, and Christians were facing loss of property and famine. In a difficult economic climate, generosity was drying up. It is understandable, then, that the rich person who converted to Christianity was an attractive source of essential income. The church would offer grand hospitality to the rich in order to secure their support—even at the expense of caring for those who needed it most.

This is favoritism at work: favoring a wealthy person (whether it be someone who has monetary wealth or wealth in power or skills) over someone who is poor.

Humanity plays favorites out of the desire to own something possessed by the rich. Churches—then and now—may profess that this is "ministry" to the wealthy. But their behavior is not about caring for the rich person's needs. It is about making sure their own needs are met by the rich person's wealth.

 *Food for Thought*

What needs do you have at work right now? To whom are you going in order to have those needs met?

_____

_____

_____

_____

_____

While James might be specifically addressing the church, this kind of behavior is also found at work. At work, we might find ourselves tempted to give our attention only to those who can help us, rather than spend time on those who need our help. As business leaders, we might find ourselves pouring a disproportionate amount of resources into winning the hearts of potential investors, at the cost of charitable giving or even fair wages for our employees. Where someone is being unfairly treated or even harassed, we might hold back from supporting them, controlled instead by the desire to keep the powerful and the successful on our side.

Jesus never acted in this way. He gave his life for the world's most needy—us. This is because he trusted wholeheartedly that God would sustain him in all he did.

 Food for Thought

Who is "poor" at your workplace? Think of the person who is often seen alone, picked on, or gossiped about. Bring to mind the groups of people who get the worst jobs, the lowest pay, or the least attention. How might you support these people today?

_____

_____

_____

_____

_____

_____

Prayer

Pause for a few moments of silence to reflect on what you've just studied. Then offer a prayer, either spontaneous or by using the following:

Jesus Christ, fair and just and loving God,

Thank you for never discriminating against me. Forgive me, as I have discriminated against others. Forgive me, as I have shown favoritism to others to provide for my needs. Again, I choose to place my trust in you. I bring my needs to you today. [List them below.]

_____

_____

_____

_____

Thank you that you poured out your life for the poor and needy, and that even now you are pouring yourself out for me as I come to you in need.

In your name I pray, amen.

Lesson #2: Two Arguments against Favoritism (James 2:5–8)

James offers three arguments against the kind of discrimination we see in this passage. The first is that showing favoritism to the rich is actually a sign of lacking trust in God. "Do you with your acts of favoritism really believe in our glorious Lord Jesus Christ?" (James 2:1, NRSV). By playing favorites in order to provide for our needs, we demonstrate a lack of trust that God will provide. James's readers were oscillating between trusting God to provide and trying to secure what they needed from their wealthy converts. When we trust God to provide for our needs, however, our desire to have our needs met by the rich person's wealth will fade away.

By comparison, the poor must trust God for their needs. Greater trust leads to stronger faith and deeper love for God. Because of this, we might be tempted to think that there is something inherently noble or right about being poor, that the poor are somehow better than the rich. On the contrary, James explains in verse 5 that it is because they have greater faith and love for God. "Has not God chosen those who are poor in the eyes of the world to be *rich in faith* and to inherit the kingdom he promised *those who love him*?" (emphasis added).

Lacking the means to depend on themselves, and lacking the means to curry favor with the rich, the poor in the church of James's day learned to depend on the provision of God alone. Having so little, they found everything in their heavenly Father, the giver of all good things. Why, then, should Jesus' followers discriminate against the ones who respond to God's love with such a deep love for him?

Food for Thought

Read aloud Matthew 5:1–10, the beatitudes from Jesus' famous Sermon on the Mount. What does this passage reveal to you about who is blessed by God?

_____

_____

_____

_____

_____

_____

_____

_____

James's second argument against wealth discrimination is straightforward—it doesn't make any sense! Ironically, currying favor with the rich isn't even an effective strategy for tapping their wealth. "Is it not the rich who are exploiting you? Are they not the ones who are dragging you into court?" (2:6). After the fawning is over, the rich have much greater ability to dispose of the poor than the poor have to weasel money out of the rich. Have you ever suffered from the arbitrary power of rich people or organizations yourself, whether at work, in civic life, or in the legal system? Trusting God is not only more faithful, it is more productive.

Considering the way we see wealth at work in the world around us, why do wealthy people continue to attract our attention so much? In the same way a Venus flytrap attracts a fly, we are attracted by the scent of "There might be something in it for me."

Wealthy people attract us because we get confused into thinking they might become our provider. Again, we find ourselves back at the message of James 1:5—*God* gives generously to all—and 1:17—every good and perfect gift is *from God*. The rich man isn't your provider, God is. The logical response is to favor him and the desires of his heart. It's only common sense.

 Food for Thought

Do you ever find yourself attracted to spending time, energy, or resources to gain favor with someone in your workplace? What do you imagine that person has to offer you? Is this something God could offer you?

_____

_____

_____

_____

_____

_____

_____

_____

Prayer

Pause for a few moments of silence to reflect on what you've just studied. Then offer a prayer, either spontaneous or by using the following:

Father God,

Help me to see the poor with your eyes. Help me to love the
poor with your heart. Break off from me any attraction I
might have to those who do not love or support me. Help
me to see the riches of the world for what they truly are.
Help me to see the riches of your kingdom in all their glory.
Help me to keep my affection fixated on you, the One who
loves me, always and forever.

In Christ's name I pray, amen.

Lesson #3: Favoritism Isn't Love (James 2:8–13)

James moves to his third and final argument against favoring the
wealthy and neglecting the poor—because it breaks the law of love.

In this passage, James takes his readers back to an Old Testament law: "Love your neighbor as yourself" (Lev. 19:18). This is
the same verse heralded by Jesus as the second great commandment (see Matt. 22:37–40). James calls this the "royal law," the
law of the kingdom of God. This law is like a red carpet rolled
out for Christ, which he walks upon to the cross. As we follow it,
so too are we following him.

James highlights this law, or "commandment," because favoritism is in direct violation of it. In showing partiality to the rich,
the church was looking after its own needs and not loving the
poor and meeting their needs.

Perhaps we could say that by treating the rich in this way, we are
loving them as our neighbors. However, we would then have to
deny that the poor are also our neighbors. Our resources are limited. Consider the effect favoring the rich has on the nearby poor.

While the wealthy are showered with praise, the poor feel they have little to be praised for. While the rich are greeted with gifts, the poor—who have so little—receive nothing. While the rich eat lavish food, the poor—who always eat simply—eat simply again.

 Food for Thought

Think now about those you work alongside. Have you recently been favoring a colleague who is rich (be it in power, talent, monetary wealth, ability, or popularity)? As you have done this, how might you have neglected to love a colleague who is poor?

_____

_____

_____

_____

_____

_____

Breaking this law has serious consequences. James tells us that breaking this one law in effect breaks God's whole law. The reason for this is that God's laws are not disparate elements, like bullet points in a list. They are rivers and streams that flow from one source—the mercy of God. As we break any law, we break away from the mercy of God (James 2:13).

If we don't want to be lawbreakers, and instead desire to follow God with a renewed vitality at work, we would do well to start by showing mercy to the poor and weak we come across every day. Perhaps we might have a coffee today with an unpopular colleague? Stand up for the marginalized, the gossiped about, the harassed? Share our skills with the flailing intern? Buy lunch for the co-worker we know could never pay us back? Help the one who desperately needs help? Love the one who desperately needs love?

Food for Thought

How will you show mercy to a forgotten, poor, or weak colleague today?

_____

_____

_____

_____

_____

Prayer

Pause for a few moments of silence to reflect on what you've just studied. Then offer a prayer, either spontaneous or by using the following:

Father God, Father to the fatherless and defender of the widow,

I come to you today with a renewed desire to follow you, and like you, love the helpless. Change my heart—put an end to my selfish desire to pursue the powerful, win over the wealthy, and socialize with the popular. By your spirit, direct me to the poor and powerless at my work. By your Spirit, help me to meet their needs with love.

In Christ's name I pray, amen.

Chapter 4

Faith and Work(s)

Lesson #1: What Are Works? (James 2:14–17)

In this portion of the letter, James looks in detail at the relationship between faith and works or deeds. James uses the Greek word *erga*, the plural "works," rather than *ergon*, the singular "work," which has led some to believe that James isn't referring to our ordinary work or occupation, but rather to some special attempt to earn God's favor by our actions.

On the contrary, the word *works* (or *deeds* as some translations put it) refers to *all* that we do. Good works are any outputs of our lives done in obedience to God. This means anything done as an act of kindness, from sharing a meal with a hungry neighbor to paid employment, such as waiting tables or improving the sustainable yield of a rice paddy in Southeast Asia. These are all "works." James merely uses the plural form of the word to indicate that these "outputs" (these things we do as a result of our faith) are many and ongoing, not one-off events in the past.

 Food for Thought

Make a master to-do list for your workday today or tomorrow. On it, include everything you must do, from completing projects to lunch with a friend, to the e-mails you need to send, to drinking water and getting home. How could all of these be good "works" done in obedience to God?

———————————————————————————————

———————————————————————————————

———————————————————————————————

———————————————————————————————

———————————————————————————————

———————————————————————————————

———————————————————————————————

———————————————————————————————

In 2:15, the example James employs is carefully chosen to illustrate his understanding of works: a brother or sister who is in need of food and clothing receives only words of empty well-wishing from their neighbor. This is the opposite of faith in action, a "non-work." A "work" in this scenario, performed in obedience to God, would have been an action to feed and clothe this needy friend.

Through this example James highlights an idea we see throughout his whole letter—that our works should have a particular focus on meeting others' needs. One way to conceptualize works is to understand them as acts that meet the needs of others. Employment therefore is easily translated to "works" because much employment revolves around needs. Every day at work, no matter what we are employed to do, we will be presented with the opportunity to meet the needs of someone else, and in doing so, the opportunity to do "works" for God.

 *Food for Thought*

While you are at work today, be on the lookout for someone who needs your help. Or if you already know who that might be, plan ahead! How might you put your faith into action today on their behalf?

_____

_____

_____

_____

_____

_____

_____

Prayer

Pause for a few moments of silence to reflect on what you've just studied. Then offer a prayer, either spontaneous or by using the following:

> *Father God,*
>
> *You have created me for a purpose. You have set before me good works, planned in advance for me to do. Help me see the possibilities of my life. Help me, even as I work today, to see the possible ways that I might be working for you.*
>
> *In Christ's name, amen.*

Lesson #2: Can Our Work Save Us? (James 2:14–26)

James's focus on what we do, our work, has led to deep controversy over this letter. Martin Luther, leader of the Protestant Reformation, famously disliked James because he read in James 2:24, "You see that a person is justified by what he does and not by faith alone" (NRSV). To Luther, this seemed to be a contradiction to Galatians 2:16 where Paul writes, "A person is not justified by the works of the law, but by faith in Jesus Christ."

It is impossible to engage fully with this debate within the boundaries of this study. However, we will spend this lesson focusing on just one question: Is it possible to be saved (or "justified") by the work we do?

Protestant churches have historically rejected this notion, and the Roman Catholic Church has also clarified that it rejects the notion that salvation is gained by works. The grace of God, given in faith in Jesus Christ, not the works we do, is what justifies us and brings God's salvation to us.

But is James arguing against justification by faith in 2:24? To properly understand his position, we have to take the whole section on faith and works into consideration.

In James 2:14, he says, "What good is it, my brothers and sisters, if someone claims to have faith but has no deeds? Can such faith save them?" In 2:17, he answers himself, "Faith by itself, if it is not accompanied by action, is dead." We can picture faith in Christ like a garden. When our faith is alive, our garden will be producing flowers and fruits—goods or works. But if nothing is being produced, then the garden must not be alive. It is dead.

This liveliness of faith is at the heart of James's letter: faith that is alive cannot help but produce good works, just as a garden that is alive cannot help but produce flowers and fruits. James does not imagine anyone producing good works without the garden—the faith—that yields them. There can be no good works unless there is already a faith (or trust) in God. James also does not imagine anyone having a faith-garden that doesn't produce fruits. What kind of garden exists yet grows nothing? This is why James says, "Not by faith alone," because faith "alone" is no faith at all.

In the end, work alone will not save us. And neither will a so-called faith that yields no action. It is a living faith, an active faith, a working garden of faith, a faith that results in acts of obedience to its Creator, that sees us justified before our God.

 Food for Thought

Perhaps you are different from Luther and find yourself resting easy in the knowledge that you are saved. Do you ever shut out God's instruction for your life and instead follow your own path? How might the image of the "garden of faith" help to move you along from where you are now?

Prayer

Pause for a few moments of silence to reflect on what you've just studied. Then offer a prayer, either spontaneous or by using the following:

> *Father God,*
>
> *Thank you for saving me. Thank you for planting faith in me and accepting my miniscule offering of faith back to you. Grow my faith. Expand it. Breathe life into it. Help good works to flow out of it, like a flourishing garden of life that blesses all those around me, that finds its roots in you.*
>
> *In Christ's name I pray, amen.*

Lesson #3: Separating Faith and Work? (James 2:18–26)

The insight that faith always leads to practical action is, in itself, a lesson for the workplace. Since there is no scriptural divide between the spiritual life and the practical one, we can't divide our faith-life and our work-life either. To say, "Well, I believe in Jesus and go to church on Sunday, but I keep my faith out of my work" is the same as saying, "I can have faith without deeds."

Jonathan, working as a professor of psychology at a large state university, knows firsthand how hard it is to allow faith to permeate his work. Out of a department of almost one hundred faculty and staff, as far as he knew, he was one of only a few Christians. While he found it easy to practice his faith at church on Sunday, life on Monday morning was drastically different. "The work environment at the university was oppressive. It was characterized by a pressure to succeed and a self-centeredness that tainted our relationships. Everyone wanted to get ahead—in promotions, in grants, in publications." His Sunday to Monday transition was like a weekly transition between summer and winter. It was like living two different lives.

How can we put our faith into action if we find ourselves in workplaces that reward putting our needs first, exploiting other people, and neglecting love for the sake of advancement—the opposite of what James describes as good works?

 Food for Thought

Think about your own workplace. What are the differences between your understanding of faith in Christ and your experience of work? How is your behavior at work different from what your faith tells you is good?

_____

_____

_____

_____

_____

_____

_____

Think back to the "faith garden" discussed in the last lesson. A living faith results in works, acts of obedience to God. Faith and works are part of a system. They are interrelated and can't be untangled.

At times we rationalize division between our God-life and our work-life. We may say that we keep our faith out of the workplace, but the insight that faith always leads to practical action is a lesson for the workplace. Since we can't divide our spiritual life ("faith") from its practical repercussions ("works"), we cannot divide our faith-life from our employment either. Our active faith should be producing good works always—on Sunday *and* on Monday. Faith produces obedience everywhere, and that will inevitably include obedience to God at work.

 Food for Thought

How might you better allow your spiritual life to flow into your physical, working life? Think again about the differences between your experience of church and work. How would you like them to be the same? What's the first step you could take to making this a reality?

_____

_____

_____

_____

_____

_____

_____

Prayer

Pause for a few moments of silence to reflect on what you've just studied. Then offer a prayer, either spontaneous or by using the following:

Father God, God of all work,

Break down any walls I might put up that prevent your Spirit from working in my workplace. Help my faith to be just as active, just as impactful, on Monday and Tuesday and Wednesday and Thursday and Friday and Saturday as it is on Sunday. Do your work through me. Transform the place where I work. Have it worship you.

In Christ's name I pray, amen.

Chapter 5

Speaking and Listening

Lesson #1: Learning to Listen Well (James 1:19–21)

James turns to the topic of listening when he writes, "Everyone should be quick to listen" (1:19). In this he echoes the wisdom literature of the Old Testament, which prizes listening highly. "The prudent hold their tongues" (Prov. 10:19). "Even fools are thought wise if they keep silent, and discerning if they hold their tongues" (Prov. 17:28). "The wise listen to advice" (Prov. 12:15). Christians who want to live wisely need to listen well.

Learning to listen, however, is hard. It is much easier to give your opinion, to control a meeting, to be the funny one, to tell your side of the story, to let off steam, to debrief after a long hard day—much easier to crush even the sincerest intentions to listen well. Is intentional listening really worth the effort?

It is, because listening changes us. The difference between speaking and listening is that we speak to influence others, but we listen as a way to clear space for God to influence us. Interestingly, James proposes listening to others as a way to rid ourselves of evil. This works, not because others are always speaking God's word to us, but because in the act of listening we stop the anger and arrogance that prevent us from hearing and obeying God's word. Your "anger does not produce the righteousness that God desires," writes James (1:20). Instead, he calls us to "humbly accept the word planted in you, which can save you" (1:21).

 *Food for Thought*

Let's spend some time reflecting on our workplace-listening weaknesses. When do you find it hard to be a good listener? During meetings? At social functions? On Monday morning after an eventful weekend? To whom do you find it hard to listen? A particular colleague? Your boss? Make a conscious decision this week to close your mouth and leave moments of silence in those situations where you find good listening most difficult.

———————————————————————————

———————————————————————————

———————————————————————————

———————————————————————————

———————————————————————————

———————————————————————————

———————————————————————————

———————————————————————————

Listening must happen at the organizational level too. In order to succeed, businesses need to listen well to their customers, employees, investors, and local communities. Doctors listen to their patients to determine what medicine to prescribe. Freelance journalists listen to their editors to determine what kind of articles to write. Marketing executives need to listen to their intended audience to determine how best to launch a product, and so on. Listening is the only way to determine a customer's needs, and the act of meeting a customer's needs is the fuel that drives the engine of a business.

This should remind us again that the world of our employment is fertile ground for God's work. As we go about our daily tasks of listening to our customers, investors, and employees, we have the opportunity to meet the needs of those around us—and for God, in that moment of listening, to transform us. Listening changes us and can change us even as we work.

 Food for Thought

If you are working through this study in a group, take turns sharing how you feel God has been challenging you at work over the time you've been meeting together, while the others listen attentively without interruption.

_____

_____

_____

_____

_____

_____

_____

_____

Prayer

For prayer today, pray without speaking. Sit before God in silence, offering him a moment when you are listening attentively, looking for him to speak his transforming word into your life.

Lesson #2: The Impossible Quest for Holy Speech (James 3:1–8)

Speaking is the flip side of listening, and it comes as no surprise that James warns against bad speech as much as he encourages good listening. Again, James's message is in alignment with the rest of Scripture. With his words he evokes proverbs such as, "Those who guard their lips preserve their lives, but those who speak rashly will come to ruin" (Prov. 13:3), "A scoundrel plots evil, and on their lips it is like a scorching fire" (Prov. 16:27), and "The tongue has the power of life and death, and those who love it will eat its fruit" (Prov. 18:21).

The tongue is powerful. To describe its work, James utilizes some of the fiercest language found in the book: the tongue "corrupts the whole body" and "is itself set on fire by hell" (3:6). Not only is the tongue powerful, but it is also out of control. "No human being can tame the tongue," warns James (3:8).

 Food for Thought

Have you ever said something with disastrous consequences? If you could travel back in time, how would you change what you said and did in that same situation?

_____

_____

_____

_____

_____

_____

Lesson #3: Rejecting Two-Faced Behavior (James 3:9–12)

We can't travel back in time, but we can be careful not to "curse human beings, who have been made in God's likeness" (James 3:9) while at the office. Usually our curses are done in secret. Don't we ridicule our superiors, complain about our co-workers, gossip, let out our frustration on our employees, and even engage in harsh joking—and always do it when the people we're talking about aren't around? Then we smile and pretend to be friends when they're around.

This two-faced behavior is what James laments in 3:10 as he writes, "Out of the same mouth come praise and cursing. My brothers and sisters, this should not be." God transforms us inwardly as we place our faith in him. We saw in chapter 1 that he has given us a "new birth." Likewise, our inward transformation should result in a corresponding outward transformation. If we have received mercy from God, we need to become merciful to the people we work with, and that includes the way we talk about them. Nevertheless, at times that transformation, like a kite on a tree branch, finds itself snagged on our speech. We must not let a single snag (the way we talk about people) hold us back from the heights of good work overall, nor let that one spark set the whole course of our lives on fire. As impossible as it may seem, because of its power to do unbelievable harm, we need to keep our speech in check.

 Food for Thought

Identify a time at work when you almost lost control of your speech. Does your speech get the better of you around particular people? In a particular venue? At particular times of the day? The next time you are in that situation, count to ten before speaking out loud. It may seem absurd, but waiting and thinking before you act is a great first step to taking hold of the reins of the impossible tongue.

Prayer

Pause for a few moments of silence to reflect on what you've just studied. Then offer a prayer, either spontaneous or by using the following:

Jesus Christ, holy and blameless One,

Please come now and purify my speech. I am sorry I sometimes let my speech curse the people I work with. Forgive me, and as you do, replace by your Spirit my words of frustration with new words of patience, my words of anger with new words of gentleness, my words of stupidity and ignorance with new words of wisdom, my words of thoughtlessness with your words of love.

In your name I pray, amen.

Chapter 6

Me vs. You

Lesson #1: "Wisdom" vs. Peace (James 3:13–18)

Go on, treat yourself. Find yourself. Take good care of yourself. Make sure you get some "me" time. Life is short, buy the shoes. Just do it.

These are mere snippets of the "wisdom" we can sample around us today—so full of self and "stuff." How could that sort of "wisdom" ever lead to "deeds done in . . . humility" (James 3:13)? Don't humble deeds require a smallness and other-centeredness absent from the catchphrases of "me" and "mine"?

James writes to tell us that the "wisdom" that promotes ourselves as number one, that feeds our desire to consume every dish in sight, is not wisdom at all. It is merely a set of self-serving ideas that come from our own corrupt desires and from the devil (4:7). Behavior born of this "wisdom" breaks apart families and disintegrates workplace relationships. Such "wisdom" only puts us in a constant state of disruption, leaving life on earth feeling like an endless ride in a downtown taxicab, bumped around and never at rest.

 Food for Thought

Think of the catchphrases used regularly at your workplace and by your colleagues. Make a list of them and challenge yourself.

Can you find verses in Scripture that either confirm or contradict them? What would God's catchphrase be for your workplace?

_____

_____

_____

_____

_____

_____

Selfish ambition is the opposite of serving the needs of others, and while false wisdom brings disorder, true wisdom pours out goodness like fresh water on all it comes in contact with. "The wisdom that comes from heaven is first of all pure; then peace-loving, considerate, submissive, full of mercy and good fruit, impartial and sincere" (3:17). These aren't ethereal markers of a super-spiritual person. They are real, practical effects of a God-centered perspective on the world.

In verse 18, James highlights one practical effect in particu-lar—peacemaking. Where false wisdom brings disorder, true wisdom ultimately brings peace. You'll note that James uses a workplace example here—of a farmer sowing and harvesting his crop. Peacemaking is work—hard work! Regardless, as we put aside our preconceptions and accept the wisdom of God as the best direction for our lives, it is possible that this behavior will have an effect on others. This is what peacemaking is—creating an atmosphere in our homes, our churches, and our places of work where conduct that is pleasing to God can start to flourish. Where justice is possible. Where peace is in abundance. Wouldn't that be a wonderful place to work?

 *Food for Thought*

Do you have colleagues in your industry who are wise with the "wisdom that comes from heaven"? What traits from James 3:17 do you see exhibited in their lives? Be aware that this "saint" is just a regular Christian like yourself, facing the same temptations and trials you do. How might you grow to be more like these wise friends? Are you currently facing unrest at work? How might you "sow in peace" (3:18) in this situation? How might you create a space in your workplace where good conduct might start to grow?

_____

_____

_____

_____

_____

Prayer

Pause for a few moments of silence to reflect on what you've just studied. Then offer a prayer, either spontaneous or by using the following:

Jesus Christ, Prince of Peace,

Bring your peace to me now. Where I have listened to the wisdom of the world, and it has caused turmoil within me, come and bring your peace. Where those around me are chasing their dreams at the expense of others, come and bring your peace. Where there is unrest and stress in my workplace, come and bring your peace. Bring your peace, Lord, and wherever I am, bring your peace through me.

In your name I pray, amen.

Lesson #2: Ambition vs. Submission (James 4:1–10)

Graham was a leading Australian statistician, working both as a consultant and as an academic in the field, until his death from cancer in 2010. Before his passing, Robert, a junior colleague asked him for his best career advice. Graham's response took him by surprise. "He told me that for most nights in the early days, he would take home piles of work, and work late. During that time Graham's young son would sit by him at the desk, wanting to read books and play. He would concede—a little. He would give half of his attention to his work and half to his son. His advice was that he wished he had put the work down and spent the time with his son instead."

Graham's story is sad but not uncommon. Self-centered ambition drives us to chase achievement at the expense of those around us. It is this kind of ambition that causes quarrels and fights (James 4:2). We neglect our families and friends. We use others as stepping-stones to promotion, we steal credit for a co-worker's work, we shift the blame for a failed project to protect ourselves, we take advantage of someone else for our own profit, and so on. This is the definition of selfish ambition. Before our eyes dangles the carrot of our own success, our own power, our own pleasure—all of which we imagine we can get apart from God. As soon as we reach out for that, as soon as we start doing whatever it takes to get it, in our selfishness we become friends with the world and enemies of God (4:4).

This is a wretched place to be. Selfish ambition does not provide contentment or happiness or, at its ultimate end, eternal life. The solution to it all is submission to God (4:7). Whenever we decide to break off our friendship with the world—James's term for coveting what we do not possess—God is ready to offer his grace (4:6). The correct approach is to come to God in prayer with a heavy heart concerning our sin and commit to leaving our selfish ambitions for dead. "Come near to God and he will come near to you. Wash your hands, you sinners, and purify your hearts, you double-minded. Grieve, mourn and wail. Change your laughter to mourning and your joy to gloom. Humble yourselves before the Lord, and he will lift you up" (4:8–10).

 Food for Thought

Have you been chasing success at work at the expense of others, or even at the expense of following God? Come to him now in prayer and ask him for forgiveness.

_____

_____

_____

_____

_____

_____

_____

_____

As we submit to God, our behavior toward our colleagues will also change. Submission to God means submission to his perspective on the world. Our God is a God who created us in his own image (Gen. 1:27) and who sent his Son to die for all (2 Cor. 5:14). Complete submission to God, then, includes the act of putting aside our self-serving interests and working instead for the people whom God has created, pursued, and loved.

 *Food for Thought*

Do you want to rise to a position of authority and excellence? Begin by helping other workers increase their authority and excellence. Does success motivate you? Invest in the success of those around you. Think about who these people might be and where might you use that attention to detail to bring glory to God rather than yourself.

_____

_____

_____

_____

_____

_____

_____

_____

Ironically, investing in others' success may also turn out to be the best thing you can do for yourself. According to economists Elizabeth Dunn of the University of British Columbia and Michael Norton of Harvard Business School, investing in other people makes us happier than spending money on ourselves.

Prayer

Pause for a few moments of silence to reflect on what you've just studied. Then offer a prayer, either spontaneous or by using the following:

Almighty God,

I submit myself to you again today. I am sorry for pursuing my own glory and pleasure. Cleanse me of my selfishness, burn up in my heart my selfish ambition. I long to see the world the way you do. I long to free my life from meaningless pursuits and replace it all with a meaningful existence that fights for and chases after you. Turn my wrong motivations around, into a motivation to do your work.

In Christ's name I pray, amen.

Lesson #3: Slander vs. Love (James 4:11–12)

James 4:11 says, "Do not slander." What is slander? It is to speak against someone else falsely. This includes bringing a false accusation against another person, questioning another's proper authority, speaking badly about a person behind their back, and criticizing (with intent to harm) another's true talent or success. Slander is the act of speaking words that hurt. It is a manifestation of our own pride and ambition, which we saw in the last lesson is opposed by God. Slander is almost always the place where quarrelling ends up. Slander is sin.

James says, "Anyone who speaks against a brother or sister or judges them speaks against the law and judges it" (4:11). The law he is referring to is the same one he quotes in 2:8, "Love your neighbor as yourself." By speaking words that hurt, we attack our neighbor, not love them. In doing so, we exhibit through our behavior an internal decision that this great command of Jesus is worthless. We "judge" it. We have decided it is worthless to obey.

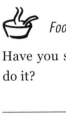 *Food for Thought*

Have you slandered someone recently at work? Why did you do it?

_____

_____

_____

_____

_____

_____

_____

Our work colleagues are our "neighbors." We are tasked with the responsibility of loving them, just as we are tasked with the responsibility of loving our friends and family. In his death on the cross, Jesus showed us what true love is—laying down our lives for other people (1 John 3:16). In love we position ourselves as less important than our neighbors. Conversely, when we slander we stand over others in a position of judgment. We elevate ourselves. Again, this breaks the law of love.

The solution to slander is humility before God. Only God can sit in judgment before someone else. Go back to James 4:7–10 where he tells us to submit ourselves, resist, wash our hands, grieve, and humble ourselves. In that place, we will find the order of the world comes right again. Rather than standing on a pedestal above our workmates, hurling insults and undue criticisms, we'll see them through the selfless perspective of Christ, the perfect place from which to come alongside them, support them, and love them.

 Food for Thought

How could you speak words of love to those you have criticized? Could you apologize in a way that undoes the wrong, rather than simply makes you feel better about it? How could you express Christ's love to them today?

_____

_____

_____

_____

_____

_____

_____

Prayer

Pause for a few moments of silence to reflect on what you've just studied. Then offer a prayer, either spontaneous or by using the following (from Phil. 2:6–8):

Jesus Christ,

You, who being in very nature God,
did not consider equality with God something to be used
to your own advantage,
who made yourself nothing,
by taking the very nature of a servant,
being made in human likeness.
And being found in appearance as a man,
humbled yourself
by becoming obedient to death—
even death on a cross!

I praise you, Lord Jesus, for you know what it is to truly love. Help me to put myself aside. Help me to love as you have loved.

In your mighty name, amen.

Chapter 7

Two Warnings for the Wealthy

Lesson #1: We Don't Control the Future (James 4:13–17)

This section of James addresses some of the business leaders of his day. These were Christians who engaged in business, could travel at will, and, most importantly, felt confident they would make money while doing so. James speaks to them with harsh words. "What is your life?" he asks. "You are a mist that appears for a little while and then vanishes" (4:14). Does James hate businesspeople?

James is not taking issue with these Christians making money, or even their desire to do so. It might seem that James is condemning business planning, even short-term planning, but neither is the case. Working hard, making a profit, planning—none of these by themselves are issues in our lives. In fact, we are responsible to use wisely the resources, abilities, and time that God gives us. The real problem is planning as if the keys to the future lay in our hands.

Most businesses are aware of the unpredictable, uncontrollable nature of the future. The annual report of any publicly traded corporation will feature a detailed section on risks the company faces, often running ten or twenty pages long. Statements such as "Our stock price may fluctuate based on factors beyond our control" make it clear that corporations are attuned to the uncertainty of the future. Why, then, is it such a difficult concept for believers to grasp? We can't control the future, not one single jot of it. God does. Yet we boast and brag about where we're headed in life, what we will achieve, and how we will succeed. "All such boasting is evil," declares James (4:16), because in doing so we imply that we are God.

 Food for Thought

Have you ever had a major setback at work due to events outside of your control? How did you react? What can you do to remain grounded the next time something like that occurs?

_____

_____

_____

_____

_____

_____

_____

What, then, might we change? We can start by being aware of the need to continually reassess, adapt, and adjust our plans. As we go about our workday—and also as we move forward with our careers—our plans should be flexible and our execution responsive to changing conditions. In one sense, this is just good business practice. In a deeper sense, however, this is a spiritual matter, because as believers we are not only subject to market conditions, but we are also subject to the leading of God. God is the only one with an understanding of our future. Therefore, it makes sense to acknowledge that it is he who leads us, which brings us back to James's exhortation to listen well. Christians at work need to listen to and interpret not only patterns in the world around them but also God's word and his unfolding guidance in their lives.

 Food for Thought

Two of the ways we can discern where God is leading us are through time spent in prayer and reading Scripture. How have you been lately at regularly practicing these spiritual disciplines? How regularly do you spend time in prayer, asking God to lead you as you work? Look at your schedule for the week. Find some times you can dedicate solely to reading his word and listening to him.

_____

_____

_____

_____

_____

_____

_____

_____

Prayer

Today, for the second time in this study, spend some time in silence, listening to God. Ask him earnestly to direct the course of your working life.

Lesson #2: We Must Not Hoard Wealth (James 5:1–4)

Once again, James reminds his readers of the importance of serving the needs of others. This time, James does it by focusing on the wicked rich. James is so certain of God's judgment awaiting these men and women that, even as their gold lusters and their cloaks are soft and new, he can already pronounce their riches as dead and decomposing. These particular folk are doomed, both for how they amassed their wealth and what they did with it. Even though these words were first written to the unbelieving rich, as followers of Jesus we can still learn two lessons from the warnings presented here.

First, for those of us who are employers, we must be especially diligent about paying our workers fairly. "Look! The wages you failed to pay the workers who mowed your fields are crying out against you" (5:4). What constitutes "fair pay" is beyond the scope of this study, but these verses are a direct indictment against failing to pay workers appropriately as a means to build our own wealth.

We must be careful that our power does not result in someone being paid unfairly. The employers of James's day had found a way to circumvent the law in order to pay their workers less. Purposeful misclassification of workers as independent contractors, inaccurate placement of someone on a pay scale, paying a woman or minority worker less for doing the same job as someone else—the Lord will hear the cries of these workers, and their employer will be subject to judgment.

 *Food for Thought*

Are you responsible for someone else's pay? Since this is such an important role in caring for another person's needs, how might you stay accountable in order to do this job fairly?

_____

_____

_____

_____

_____

_____

_____

Lesson #3: Watching Out for Self-Indulgence (James 5:5–6)

James also condemns those who "have lived on the earth in luxury and in self-indulgence" (5:5). The problem is not the actual luxury or pleasure but the diversion of wealth when others are in need. "You have fattened yourselves in the day of slaughter," James accuses (5:6). While others suffered, these rich people idled away the hours without care.

What then should those who have money do with it? Other than paying workers fairly, as we have just discussed, James doesn't say. He leaves it up to us to figure out how our wealth could be used to help people in need. One long-standing Christian tradition is frugality—making do with fewer or less luxurious goods and services. However, saving money only helps others if we use the money actively for their benefit. If we merely hoard it for ourselves, we are no better than the idle rich. John Wesley put

it this way: "Make all you can, save all you can, give all you can."
By saving all you can, he did not mean shopping for bargains or
building up a cash reserve. He meant reducing personal con-
sumption in order to use more of our resources to help others.

By this reckoning generosity not frugality is the proper attitude
toward money. One crucial element of generosity is giving away
money and doing so wisely. Yet generosity can mean spending
more rather than less, if we spend it on others. It can mean paying higher prices for services or goods produced in ways that
create social capital, environmental sustainability, or just treat-
ment of workers. Generosity can also mean investing money in
enterprises that fill unmet needs for goods and services, create
jobs, and support communities.

In today's complex economies, it is not easy to know how our de-
cisions about money will affect other people. There is an urgent
need for Christians to become more educated about economics
because, as James shows, God cares about the actual good—or
harm—that our use of money can do.

 Food for Thought

Is there any area of your spending that could be headed toward
"self-indulgence"? What are some practical ways you could become more generous instead? Are there ways, through the work
you do, that you could invest economic, social, or relational capital to benefit others?

_____

_____

_____

_____

Prayer

Pause for a few moments of silence to reflect on what you've just studied. Then offer a prayer, either spontaneous or by using the following:

Jesus Christ,

I know you will come again to judge the living and the dead. Help me to live a life that is pleasing to you. Help me to use my finances in a way pleasing to you. Help me— through the careful spending, giving, and investing of my wealth—to care for others. You are Lord over all I have. I place my income and my belongings at your feet. Use them as you will for the needs of your people.

In your name I pray, amen.

Chapter 8

A Few Final Words of Advice

Lesson #1: Have Patience (James 5:7–11)

All work moves toward a purpose. It strives to create a product, hit a target, arrive at a goal, and obtain results. Nevertheless, it doesn't get there fast. Work the world over—from droving sheep at a sheep station in the Australian outback, to filing papers at a financial institution in New York City—has to walk through the day-to-day humdrum of slow progress and continual frustration. Work requires patience, but patience can be very hard work.

What happens when impatience sets in? As investors trade stock to turn a profit, does it matter if they decide to pursue quick wealth rather than slow? Or if colleagues are working to get promoted, is it a problem if they begin to take shortcuts to position themselves well in their superior's eyes? What if a production manager, pressed to meet a looming deadline, accepts work of a lesser quality? When the pressure is on, does it matter if we get grumpy and start complaining to whoever is within hearing distance?

Of course it matters—impatience betrays a lack of trust in God. In impatience we focus on the needs of ourselves and, as a result, we neglect to meet the needs of others.

 *Food for Thought*

What do you get impatient about at work? Do you find yourself acting out as a result? How could you ask for God's help in developing patience instead?

_____

_____

_____

_____

_____

_____

In James 5:7–11, the focus is on waiting, not just for the end of a project but for the ultimate endpoint—"the Lord's coming" (5:8), when Jesus will return to judge the actions of all humanity. Until then, "be patient and stand firm," says James. Until Jesus' return, our work should serve Christ with our whole heart and a determination to never let go.

James takes Job as his inspiration. Through terrible hardship— including disaster in his work-life—he never let go of his faith. Job was suddenly without property, wealth, or family. Yet he held onto God and continued to hope in him. "You have heard of Job's perseverance and have seen what the Lord finally brought about. The Lord is full of compassion and mercy" (5:11). In the end, Job received communion with God and gifts in abundance.

Whatever we might be facing at work today—whether it be anything from the tedious daily grind of slow productivity to sudden, terrible hardship—we can be encouraged with the assurance that enduring it all with patience, looking forward to Christ's return, we *will* see his goodness come to us in the end.

 *Food for Thought*

The idea that James sets forth in 5:7–11 is not new. Read Psalm
37. What verse or verses resonate with you as an encouragement
to work with patience? Find a place to copy those verses—perhaps at your desk, on your phone or laptop, or in your diary—as
a reminder to you to continue to work well.

_____

_____

_____

_____

_____

_____

Prayer

Pause for a few moments of silence to reflect on what you've just
studied. Then offer a prayer, either spontaneous or by using the
following:

Jesus Christ,

*I humbly come before you today, knowing that I am not
always patient at work. I am sorry that I act out in my
impatience, neglecting to think of the effect it has on others.
Please forgive me. Help me in my frustration to look to the
future, my future with you. Through all things, help me to
cling to the hope I have in you, looking forward to the day
when you will bring me into your heavenly kingdom. I trust
that you who call me are faithful and that you will do it.*

In your name I pray, amen.

Lesson #2: Speak Truth (James 5:12)

Fresh out of high school, Alison was desperate to land her dream job at the local boutique bookstore. It was a book lover's paradise. "Will you be going to college in the fall?" the interviewing manager had asked. "No," she had said, choking on her answer because she knew it wasn't true. Alison had already made the conscious decision that should this question arise, she would lie—otherwise she was afraid she wouldn't be offered the job.

It was only a few weeks into her time at the bookstore before she was racked with guilt. What good work could she do there, what kind of Christian witness could she be, knowing that in just a few short months she would quit, going back on her word? She would leave them without an employee at a terribly busy time of the year. She would send them back to the expensive task of searching for someone new. All because she wanted her dream job and was determined to say whatever it took to get it.

 Food for Thought

Think back to the last few times at work you said something that wasn't true. Is there a particular person or a particular situation that seems to trigger you to lie? What is stopping you from telling the truth in this situation?

_____

_____

_____

_____

_____

Imagine something completely different: a workplace where everyone always spoke the truth, a workplace where not a single person lied in their job interview—not simply avoiding lying, but where everyone provided their listeners with the most accurate information at all times. Imagine a workplace without fear of broken promises or fraud. Imagine a world where sellers always offered clear data about their product, where both parties involved in any transaction were equally informed, and where bosses never failed to give credit where credit was due.

Even if this scenario seems distant, as Christians we are called to be the initial spark of it, like the first match struck within a world enveloped by the darkness of dishonesty. "Do not swear—not by heaven or by earth or by anything else," says James in 5:12, evoking Jesus' words from Matthew 5:34–37. James urges this, not because swearing an oath is evil in itself, but because believers should not need to. We should be known as people who keep our word without resorting to linguistic trickery. Our standard should be that our yes means yes and our no means no (James 5:12). It's a call to a life of truthfulness, unwavering and unfailing, a life of truth that requires no oath to validate it.

 Food for Thought

Could you do your job, as it is right now, in a workplace where everyone always spoke the truth? What would be drastically different? Could you still be successful at your job?

_____

_____

_____

_____

_____

_____

_____

_____

Prayer

Pause for a few moments of silence to reflect on what you've just studied. Then offer a prayer, either spontaneous or by using the following:

> *Jesus Christ,*
>
> *You are the Way, the Truth, and the Life. Cleanse my speech. Put a stop to the lies I use to impress or to get what I want. Help me to be honest at work today. Help me to live a life characterized by truth. Help me to become known for my honesty at work. Help me, through all of this, to glorify you.*
>
> *In your name I pray, amen.*

Lesson #3: Get Specific (James 5:13–18)

Jack worked as an account executive at a market research firm, a job he was good at and that he enjoyed—apart from the frequent outbursts of aggression that came from his overworked, overly stressed supervisor. One particular morning, Jack arrived at work to find he was the only one there. As he sat alone in their huge open plan office, he looked over at his supervisor's empty desk and began to pray, "Let that desk be surrounded by good words today and friendly conversation." James would have loved Jack's prayer, because Jack was *getting specific.*

Romans, Ephesians, Philippians, Colossians, 1 and 2 Thessalonians, Hebrews—all of these epistles end with a reminder for their readers to pray, pray, pray. James exhorts us to be specific: "Is anyone among you in trouble? . . . Is anyone happy? . . . Is anyone among you sick?" (5:13–14). James is urging his readers to pray, specifically, and in all kinds of specific situations.

It's strange how reluctant we are at times to get specific with God. We pray using grandiose language and spiritual speech. We feel comfortable praying, "Our Father, who art in heaven, hallowed be thy name." But if we thought for a moment that "give us today our daily bread" was a prayer for actual, physical bread, we might find ourselves choking a little on the words.

James reminds us that we should be bringing the actual state of our lives, complete with our very real needs, before God. "Lord, help my bookstore to sell enough books today" is a wonderful, acceptable prayer to God. "I've made a mistake. Help me as I go and speak to my superior" is a first-class prayer.

We can turn to God with every issue, person, need, fear, and question that arises as we work. Jack never forgets that day he prayed because, for the first time ever, the entire staff surrounded his supervisor's desk and chatted together as friends. Our God is a God who answers prayers cried out from the living and breathing situations of everyday life.

 Food for Thought

What are the real needs you are facing today at work? Spend a few moments now praying for those needs. Get specific! Remember, we have a God who is the source of every good and perfect gift (1:17) and who gives wisdom generously to all (1:5).

_____

_____

_____

_____

_____

_____

_____

_____

One of the areas in which James gets specific for our prayer life is the area of confession. He exhorts us to confess our sins to one another, so that we might be healed (5:16). These words— "Confess your sins _to each other_ and pray _for each other_"—are all-important. The underlying assumption here is that we sin against each other, not just against God. If we think about our experience at work, this is especially true. As we face pressure to perform and have limited time, we act without thinking or listening. We shoot each other down, we compete unfairly, we hog resources, we leave messes for others to clean up, and we take out our frustrations on our colleagues. We wound and get wounded. Soon enough, our sin breeds sickness among the very people God has given us to love.

Yet what does our bad behavior have to do with prayer? When we wrong someone, the temptation is to leave our apology tucked neatly away in private prayer. If we cut a colleague down to size, diminishing some achievement we're jealous of, or unjustly criticize someone's performance, not only do we need to go to God, we need to go to our co-worker. Confessing. Saying sorry.

Seeking forgiveness. These are the prayer-filled acts of a community that will find healing and wholeness within itself.

 Food for Thought

Think of the people with whom you work most closely. Ask God to reveal any wrongdoing for which you need to make amends. After some time of thoughtful reflection, go to your colleague and humbly confess your sin. Also, if you have been working through this study with a group, think carefully now over whether there is any sin you need to confess to those sitting before you.

_____

_____

_____

_____

_____

_____

_____

Prayer

Pause for a few moments of silence to reflect on what you've just studied. Then offer a prayer, either spontaneous or by using the following:

Father God,

I know that you care about the specifics of my life. With that in mind, I bring to you now my specific needs at work. [List them below.]

_____

_____

_____

_____

Lord, I also ask you to give me boldness as I seek to make amends with those I have wronged around me. Soften my heart. Help me to never be too stubborn to say that I'm sorry. Lord, by the power of your Spirit, help me to maintain good relationships with my workmates. In this broken world, help my workplace to be an oasis of spiritual health.

In Christ's name I pray, amen.

Conclusion: Watch for the Wanderer (James 5:19–20)

Some years ago, Jen was working as a sales assistant for a small, local company. One of their recent hires was Luke, fresh out of high school, a sweet and naive Christian kid who was loved by all the staff. Slowly emerging from the supervision of his parents, Luke started to experiment with a lifestyle different from the one he knew—one that included soft and, not too much later, hard drugs.

"I wish I could say I warned Luke of the path he was taking," recalls Jen. "But I never did. I just watched it happen. I saw the photos online. I saw the weight he was losing. I was afraid of confronting him. Why? Because I wanted to be his friend and not his 'parent.' I made a huge mistake. I still feel sad whenever he comes to mind." Jen never saw Luke saved "from death" (5:20). The last she heard, he was still out partying, actively hurting his life, far from following Jesus Christ.

 Food for Thought

If Luke were your colleague, what would you have said to him about the direction he was taking with his life?

_____

_____

_____

_____

_____

_____

_____

James's exhortation is to strengthen one another, to build each other up. Everything we have learned in James's letter points to this one outcome: *We are here to serve the needs of others.* And everything we have learned grows from a single seed: *Entrusting our lives to God.* When we have an opportunity to serve others, we can trust God to help us. We shouldn't make the mistake Jen did. As we listen, as we pray, as we consider others before ourselves, God will give us the words to be gentle. And he will use our humble efforts to "cover over a multitude of sins" (5:20).

We might think that only pastors are qualified to engage in spiritual conversations like this. Notice, however, that James was not addressing church leaders in these verses. He was writing to readers like us. From Monday to Friday, from nine o'clock to five, we are the nearest, most present pastor our co-workers have got. Trusting in God, we must serve their needs and not neglect to guide the wandering sheep back into the fold. Jesus knew that saving someone's life is the greatest act of service we will ever do.

 Food for Thought

Ask God to bring to mind the people in your workplace whose lives are falling apart. Ask God to show you how to bring his love to each of them. If you have been following this study with a group of work colleagues, spend some time now asking how you might continue to keep one another accountable, protecting one another from getting lost along the way.

Think back over all we've studied. How might you summarize the book of James to a friend who has never read it? What is the "big idea" of James? In the end, what do you think James says about how we should work?

What changes have you seen come about in your life and work over the course of this study? What areas are you still working on? What might you ask your friends to pray for, for you and for your work, in the coming months?

_____

_____

_____

_____

Prayer

Pause for a few moments of silence to reflect on what you've just studied. Then offer a prayer, either spontaneous or by using the following:

Father God, giver of all good things,

Thank you for this study and thank you for your word. May it penetrate my thinking and influence my doing. May I continue every day to trust in you more and more. May I continue to work for the benefit of others and see their lives transformed as a result. Every day that I work for you, may I keep running—running for the prize, running to be with you forever. I look forward to the day when my work on this earth is complete and at last I see you face to face, to the day you'll say to me, "Well done, good and faithful servant."

In Christ's name I pray, amen.

Wisdom for Using This Study in the Workplace

Community within the workplace is a good thing and a Christian community within the workplace is even better. Sensitivity is needed, however, when we get together in the workplace (even a Christian workplace) to enjoy fellowship time together, learn what the Bible has to say about our work, and encourage one another in Jesus' name. When you meet at your place of employment, here are some guidelines to keep in mind:

- *Be sensitive to your surroundings.* Know your company policy about having such a group on company property. Make sure not to give the impression that this is a secret or exclusive group.

- *Be sensitive to time constraints.* Don't go over your allotted time. Don't be late to work! Make sure you are a good witness to the others (especially non-Christians) in your workplace by being fully committed to your work during working hours and doing all your work with excellence.

- *Be sensitive to the shy or silent members of your group.* Encourage everyone in the group and give them a chance to talk.

- *Be sensitive to the others by being prepared.* Read the Bible study material and Scripture passages and think about your answers to the questions ahead of time.

These Bible studies are based on the *Theology of Work Bible Commentary*. Besides reading the commentary, please visit the Theology of Work website (www.theologyofwork.org) for videos, interviews, and other material on the Bible and your work.

Leader's Guide

Living Word. It is always exciting to start a new group and study. The possibilities of growth and relationship are limitless when we engage with one another and with God's word. Always remember that God's word is "living and active, sharper than any two-edged sword" (Heb. 4:12). When you study his word, it should change you.

A Way Has Been Made. Please know that you and each person joining your study have been prayed for by people you will probably never meet but who share your faith. And remember that it is "the LORD who goes before you. He will be with you; he will not fail you or forsake you. Do not fear or be dismayed" (Deut. 31:8). As a leader, you need to know that truth. Remind yourself of it throughout this study.

Pray. It is always a good idea to pray for your study and those involved weeks before you even begin. It is recommended that you pray for yourself as leader, your group members, and the time you are about to spend together. It's no small thing you are about to start and the more you prepare in the Spirit, the better. Apart from Jesus, we can do nothing. Remain in him and you will "bear much fruit" (John 15:5). It's also a good idea to have trusted friends pray and intercede for you and your group as you work through the study.

Spiritual Battle. Like it or not, the Bible teaches that we are in the middle of a spiritual battle. The enemy would like nothing more than for this study to be ineffective. It would be part of his scheme to have group members not show up or engage in any discussion. His victory would be that your group passes time together going through the motions of just another Bible study. You, as a leader, are a threat to the enemy as it is your desire to lead people down the path of righteousness (as taught in Proverbs). Read Ephesians 6:10–20 and put your armor on.

Scripture. Prepare before your study by reading the selected Scripture verses ahead of time.

Chapters. Each chapter contains three lessons. As you work through the lessons, keep in mind the particular chapter theme in connection with the lessons. These lessons are designed so that you can go through them in thirty minutes each.

Lessons. Each lesson has teaching points with their own discussion questions. This format should keep the participants engaged with the text and one another.

Food for Thought. The questions at the end of the teaching points are there to create discussion and deepen the connection between each person and the content being addressed. You know the people in your group and should feel free to come up with your own questions or adapt the ones provided to best meet the needs of your group. Again, this would require some preparation beforehand.

Opening and Closing Prayers. Sometimes prayer prompts are given before and usually after each lesson. These are just suggestions. You know your group and the needs present, so please feel free to pray accordingly.

Bible Commentary. The Theology of Work series contains a variety of books to help you apply the Scriptures and Christian faith to your work. This Bible study is based on the *Theology of Work Bible Commentary*, which examines what the Bible says about work. This commentary is intended to assist those with theological training or interest to conduct in-depth research into passages or books of Scripture.

Video Clips. The Theology of Work website (www.theologyofwork.com) provides good video footage of people from the marketplace highlighting teaching on work from every book of the Bible. It would be great to incorporate some of these videos into your teaching time.

Enjoy Your Study! Remember that God's word does not return void—ever. It produces fruit and succeeds in whatever way God has intended it to succeed.

> "So shall my word be that goes out from my mouth;
>   it shall not return to me empty,
> but it shall accomplish that which I purpose,
>   and shall succeed in the thing for which I sent it." (Isa. 55:11)

Explore what the Bible has to say about work, book by book.

THE BIBLE AND YOUR WORK
Study Series

THEOLOGY OF WORK PROJECT